Ti in Salem

By Jeffrey Wallis

HOUGHTON MIFFLIN   BOSTON

A Puritan Village

In 1692 life was difficult in Salem Village, Massachusetts. Puritan families grew all of their own food. They made their clothing. Everyone worked hard to survive.

Puritans were serious about their religion. The law said that everyone must go to church. Everyone had to follow the church rules. The church leaders punished people who did not follow the rules. When something bad happened to a person, the Puritans said it was a punishment from God.

This is a Puritan home in Salem Village, Massachusetts.

This is a picture of a Puritan family.

The devil was real to Puritans. The Puritans believed the devil tried to make people do bad things. They believed the devil tried hardest with weak people. The Puritans believed that the people who worked for the devil were witches. It was a sin to use witchcraft. Witchcraft is the use of magic and spells. The Puritans punished people who used witchcraft with death.

Puritan children lived like adults. They were to work hard and be quiet. They worked hard in the fields, in the home, and at school. Puritan children were not allowed to play. They read the Bible and other books. The books warned them about evil.

Samuel Parris

In 1689 a new minister came to Salem Village. He was Samuel Parris. Some people welcomed him. Some did not. Parris told the people that the devil was in Salem Village.

Suddenly, the Puritans were worried about their community. There were American Indian attacks on the village. Some people got a serious disease called smallpox. Crops died in the fields. The Puritans were afraid. They thought God was angry with them.

Samuel Parris had a daughter named Betty. She was 9 years old. He also had a niece. Her name was Abigail, and she was 11 years old. The girls and their friends met to listen to stories. The stories were told by Tituba, a slave in Parris's home. Tituba was from the island of Barbados. She told stories of witchcraft and devils. These stories were exciting to the Puritan girls.

Betty, Abigail, and their friends began to act in strange ways. Sometimes the girls fell to the floor. They rolled and screamed. The village doctor said they were not sick. He said the girls were bewitched and were under a spell.

Betty and Abigail listened to Tituba's stories of witchcraft and devils.

Witchcraft!

In Salem, witchcraft was a crime. People wanted to know about the girls. Who had bewitched them? At first, the girls did not want to talk. Then the girls talked. They blamed three women: Tituba, Sarah Good, and Sarah Osborne. Were Tituba, Sarah Good, and Sarah Osborne witches?

The people of Salem believed that the three women were witches. The people did not respect these women. Sarah Osborne was old. She did not go to church. Sarah Good was homeless, and she talked quietly to herself sometimes. Some people thought that those words were really magic spells.

Many people were called witches in Salem.

This woman was arrested for witchcraft.

Judges questioned the three women. Sarah Good and Sarah Osborne said they were innocent. But Tituba confessed. She said she was guilty.

Tituba, Sarah Good, and Sarah Osborne went to jail in Boston. The conditions in jail were bad. Two months later, Sarah Osborne died in jail.

The Trials

More and more villagers said other people were witches. The accused people went on trial for witchcraft. Were they witches? Some were important and respected people in the village. For example, someone said 71-year-old Rebecca Nurse did witchcraft. Rebecca was kind and generous. Someone said George Burroughs did witchcraft too. George was once a church minister. Some of the villagers began to ask, "Are all of these people really witches?"

The accused people went on trial for witchcraft.

A girl has a shaking fit at the trial of an accused witch.

By the end of May 1692, more than 200 people of Salem were in jail. Why did the judges think that these 200 people were really witches? The judges allowed the accusers to blame specters, ghost-like images of the accused people. A person could be in one place and a specter of the person in another place. This explained why the accused people did not have to be near the victim to do harm. Accusers said the specters pinched, burned, or choked them.

The judges and people watched the young girls scream and roll on the floor. Everybody believed that the girls were suffering. Probably, the girls were victims of hysteria. This means that they were very excited and could not calm down. Hysteria could explain their strange behavior.

The Trial of Sarah Good
March 1, 1692

The court asked Sarah Good the following questions at her trial:

What evil spirit have you familiarity [are you friendly] with?
None.

Have you made no contract [an agreement] with the devil?
No.

Why do you hurt these children?
I do not hurt them. I scorn [reject] it.

Why did you go away muttering from Mr. Parris's house?
I did not mutter, but I thanked him for what he gave my child.

What creature [evil] do you employ [use] then?
No creature. I am falsely accused.

Sarah Good was hanged on July 19, 1692.

The court says that this woman is a witch.

William Phips was the Governor of Massachusetts. He set up a special court. The court asked accused people to confess. They had to say they worked for the devil. If they agreed to say this, then they would not be hanged. Forty-seven people said they worked for the devil. They were freed.

The people who did not confess went to trial. The court said they were all witches. At first, the court said Rebecca Nurse was innocent. But then the girls screamed and rolled on the floor. The court said Rebecca Nurse was guilty. The guilty were hanged. The court hanged about 19 people.

Giles Corey was not hanged, but he was killed. He did not answer any questions at his trial. The court told the sheriff to pile stones on Giles until he answered. He did not answer. After two days, Giles died. The stones crushed him.

Final Words

Bridget Bishop, 60 years old.
Was hanged June 10, 1692. She said,
"I am no witch. I am innocent."

Rebecca Nurse, 71 years old and hearing impaired.
Was hanged July 19, 1692. She said,
"Oh Lord, help me!
My life now lies in your hands."

Elizabeth Howe, 57 years old.
Was hanged July 19, 1692. She said,
"God knows I am innocent..."

George Jacobs, 72 years old.
Was hanged August 19, 1692. He said,
"I am falsely accused. I never did it."

Martha Carrier, mother of 5 children.
Was hanged August 19, 1692. She said,
"It is shameful that you should mind [listen to] these folks [people]
that are out of their wits [not thinking clearly]."

An End to Madness

Increase Mather was a Boston minister. In October 1692, Mather spoke out. Mather's writings convinced the Governor to stop the special court.

Many other people were not happy with the trials, either. Governor Phips agreed. He stopped the trials. Phips said, "many innocent persons might otherwise perish [die]."

Increase Mather

Governor Phips

In May 1693, the accused people in jail were freed. The Salem witchcraft trials ended. But crops still died in the fields. People still got sick. The Puritans thought these problems were a punishment from God. This time the punishment was for hanging innocent people. So the people had a day of prayer in 1697.

The people forced Samuel Parris to leave Salem Village in 1697. A new minister arrived. His name was Joseph Green. Joseph Green wanted to bring peace again to Salem Village.

A woman condemned as a witch is going to her hanging.

This memorial honors the people who were killed during the Salem witch trials.

> It were better that ten suspected witches should escape than that one innocent person should be condemned.

—Reverend Increase Mather

In 1711 lawmakers understood that the witch trials were wrong. They wanted to correct things. The lawmakers gave money to the families of the people who had gone to jail. Then the lawmakers began to admit that innocent people had died.

In the end, 25 people died because of the Salem witch trials. Most of the people were hanged. Historians still do not understand why the witch hysteria happened. But the American people learned a lesson. No one in America was killed for being a witch ever again.

Glossary

accused blamed for something illegal or wrong

accuser person who puts blame on someone for doing something illegal or wrong

condemn to judge someone guilty of a crime

guilty/guilt did the crime

hanged put to death by hanging with a rope around the neck

hysteria mental illness causing problems in the body

innocent/innocence did not do the crime

specter a ghost-like image

witchcraft use of magic and spells; thought to be the work of the devil